MEXICAN FAVORITES
21 TRADITIONAL RECIPES

MAMA'S LEGACY SERIES
VOLUME V — 7TH EDITION

BY NANCY N. WILSON

MEXICAN FAVORITES
21 Traditional Recipes
Mama's Legacy Series

Volume V (7th Edition) – May 2021
ISBN: 978-1-7330941-8-4
© Blurtigo Holdings, LLC
First Published 2012 in the United States of America

DEDICATION

Dedicated to my four amazing children,
Whitney, Brooke, Bryce, and Brock . . . and their father,
Robert (Buzz) Wilson
Each was willing to at least try everything that I prepared - experiments
and all. There were more than a few times that we tossed the dinner
in the garbage and opted for our family default dinner,
pancakes and scrambled eggs.

It is also dedicated
to my dear mother-in-law, Charlotte.
She introduced me to the wonderful world of *creative cooking*. It was
because of her encouragement that I was able to develop the confidence
to test my cooking wings and learn to fly!

Thank You

… for buying my book.
If you enjoy it, please take a minute and post
a review on Amazon
Mexican Food – 21 Traditional Recipes

For a complete list of my published books,
please, visit my Author's Page…
http://amazon.com/author/nancywilson

Nancy N. Wilson

Please, visit my websites
https://mamaslegacycookbooks.com
https://nancynwilson.com

Please help me continuously improve my books.
If you find errors or omissions or have a problem with a recipe,
please, contact me immediately at wilsonemarketing@gmail.com,
so that I can make the necessary corrections.

TABLE OF CONTENTS

INTRODUCTION

Dear Friends,

Welcome to *Mexican Favorites*, *Volume V* of the *Mama's Legacy Cookbook Series.*

This series was created in honor of all the wonderful women in my life who not only taught me *how* to cook but also shared with me their *love of cooking.*

Writing cookbooks has been a life-long dream of mine. I have a great passion for well-prepared, delicious food, and hopefully, this series will inspire you to stretch your creative cooking wings and begin to build your collection of recipes that can be shared with others.

I have been collecting recipes for over 60 years. The sources are numerous – beginning with my mother, then friends, colleagues, church groups, and a few updated versions of my recipes from the Internet. Other origins include old cookbooks going back to my early married years, recipes found in product packaging, and magazines that I have kept in a box in my pantry for eons.

Many were copied exactly from the paper on which they were originally written; some have morphed a little over the years, and some are newer versions of long-held recipes that have been passed from friend to friend to friend.

The *21 Traditional Recipes* in this volume range from very easy to easy, with only a couple that are slightly more difficult. The recipes are traditional Mexican food as commonly prepared in Southern Arizona. There is a little taste of everything from my own **Homemade Tacos** to **Spicy Chicken Enchiladas Verdes** from a small town in Mexico to **Creamy Margaritas** and **Flan** (a very tasty traditional dessert).

This is the only ethnic cookbook of the series, but I had to include it. Mexican food was an integral part of my youth and was the only "eating out" experience I knew until I left my small hometown in Southern Arizona to attend college.

In our little community, there were two restaurants, The Star Café, and Shorty's Mexican Food Café. My girlfriends and I ate at Shorty's once or twice a week from the time we could drive until we parted ways after high school graduation. Those were the days when you could buy a full meal and a coke for under $1.00.

Since that time, Mexican Food has been and will always be very high on my list of favorite foods when it is the real thing, not Tex-Mex or mildly flavored wannabe imitations. Unfortunately, authentic Mexican food is sometimes hard to find. That is the main reason I learned to make it myself and wanted to share these recipes with you.

I hope that well-prepared, delicious food is one of your great pleasures in life and that you will find pleasure in using the recipes in this book as much as I found in sharing them with you.

All the best,

Nancy N. Wilson

P. S. I would love to hear about your cooking adventures. Please send me stories. Your favorite recipes are also welcome if you feel like sharing. If I use them in future cookbooks, I will give you credit. You can contact me at wilsonemarketing@gmail.com.

COOKING TIPS AND GLOSSARY

PREPARATION TIPS

Irritation from Chili Peppers
Wear rubber gloves or even small plastic bags over your hands. Don't touch your face or rub your eyes while handling hot peppers. Slit the chili lengthwise, rinse under running water, remove and discard the stem, membranes, and seeds. Chop or slice as directed in the recipe. Wash hands and utensils thoroughly with hot, soapy water afterward. If your mouth is on fire, try a spoonful of sugar or a bit of salt and lime juice. The heat of a chili lasts six minutes before it dissipates.

Avoiding Tears with Onions
When cutting an onion, light a candle and place it near your work area. The flame diminishes the potency of the chemical within the onion that causes you to cry.

Shredding Beef, Chicken or Pork
When beef, chicken, or pork has been cooked until fork-tender, it's ready to be shredded. Remove from pan, take two forks and tear the meat apart until it is in smaller than bite-sized pieces. Use in tacos, enchiladas, or any other dish that needs shredded meat.

Warming Tortillas
Wrap fresh corn or flour tortillas in a clean towel – be sure it is closed well. Place in the microwave for about a minute per dozen. Requires less time if you're using fewer tortillas. Leave the tortillas in the towel to keep them warm until you serve them.

All dried red chilies are best if deveined, seeded, and soaked in just enough hot water to cover them for about an hour. Afterward, put them in the blender with the water and add them to your recipe.

It is then combined with tomatoes, onions, chilies, and spices and served with chips or saltine crackers as an appetizer.

Blistering and Peeling Chilies for Chili Rellenos
With a gas stove, you can lay the chilies over the open flame and char skins well, turning with tongs occasionally. The more charred they are, the easier it is to remove the skins. Put charred chilies into a plastic bag, close it and let it stand for 30 minutes to an hour. Remove chilies from the bag, place them under running water and remove the skin, veins, and seeds.

With an electric stove, you will have to char chilies under the broiler.

Using Canned Chilies
When using Canned Chilies or Chile Peppers, be sure to rinse them, remove seeds and stems, and pat dry with paper towels. From there, you can use them as you would fresh chilies that have been blistered in Mexican food recipes.

Stuffing Chilies
After the skin, stems and seeds have been removed from a charred fresh chili, or a whole chili straight from the can, make a slit in one side. Stuff with an appropriately sized piece of Monterey Jack cheese. The chili is now ready to be dipped in egg batter and fried.

GLOSSARY OF FOODS

Achiote
A bright red paste made from ground annatto seeds, spices, and lime juice or vinegar. It originated in the Yucatan and has been used by the Maya on fish, chicken, and pork for centuries.

Avocados
Delicate, delicious, and healthy fruits that are used to make guacamole or sliced and served as a garnish to many Mexican food meals. They are oval-shaped, with either a dark green, rough skin or a smooth medium-green skin. They must be used when they are slightly soft. Skin and peel, remove seed and use as directed in the recipe.

Burritos
Made using large, warmed flour tortillas. They are stuffed with guacamole, tomatoes, onions, beans, cheese, and either carne asada (grilled, marinated steak), shredded beef or chicken, carnitas (pork), or fish.

Carne Asada
Made from skirt or flank steak, marinated in lime and orange juice with oregano, salt, and onions. It is grilled in strips over a very hot fire, then diced and served in either soft tacos or burritos with all the traditional Mexican food condiments.

Carnitas
Originated in the state of Michoacan are made from pork simmered in fruit juices. Sometimes carnitas are baked in the oven; sometimes they are deep-

fried. They're served in either soft tacos or burritos with an array of Mexican condiments.

Ceviche
Made from raw fish, marinated until "cooked" in lime juice.

Chicharrones (Chicharron)
Deep-fried pork rinds. They're a favorite snack in Mexico (eaten like potato chips).

Chimichangas
Deep-fried meat-filled burritos.

Cilantro
Also known as coriander, is an herb used all over Mexico to jazz up salsa and other dishes. Its lively green color and equally lively flavor are a great enhancement to many dishes!

Dried Beans
To make frijoles (refried beans) put the desired quantity of dried kidney or black beans in a large pan. Cover with water and soak overnight. Drain and rinse. Add more water, to almost double the volume of beans. Cook until tender, season and serve.

Enchiladas
Made from corn tortillas, lightly fried in oil, then stuffed with cheese, onions, and most frequently, shredded beef or chicken. They can be vegetarian, or stuffed with pork, shrimp, or lobster. They are then rolled, heated, and smothered in sauce, topped with melted cheese and sometimes sour cream

Fajitas
A fun, festive dish made with marinated steak, chicken, shrimp, or mushrooms. They are then grilled on a sizzling hot skillet or comal with onions, tomatoes, bell peppers, and other chilies and served with flour tortillas burrito-style.

Flautas
Made from either corn or flour tortillas, filled with shredded beef or chicken, rolled into a thin cylinder and deep-fried, and often topped with guacamole.

Margaritas
Are the national drink of Mexico. Made usually from equal parts tequila, Cointreau, and fresh lime juice, they are served either blended with ice or on the rocks in a salt-rimmed glass.

Masa
Made of dried corn kernels, ground and mixed with water and a little ground limestone. It is a thick dough that is then flattened into patties for tortillas, or stuffed with meat and spices or fruit to make tamales.

Mexican Cheese
Mexicans do not use yellow cheese! For dishes calling for melted cheese, either Queso Monterey (Jack Cheese) or Queso Chihuahua are used. For a pungent, drier cheese to use as a garnish for tacos, guacamole, and salads, Queso Fresco is a great choice.

Mole Sauce
A dark sauce made from chilies, nuts, spices, fruits, vegetables, chocolate, and seasonings. It is difficult to make and takes a skilled hand, lots of time, and great care. It is served as a sauce in beef and chicken dishes for special occasions and holidays in Mexico. Mole Poblano, Mole Verde, Pipian and Adobo are some other variations of mole.

Menudo
A robust, fairly spicy soup that is used to cure hangovers. (Does it work? I have no idea.) The key ingredients are tripe, hominy, onions, and spices.

Salsas or Salsa
Served at almost every Mexican food meal, usually as an appetizer with chips. It's also used to jazz up everything from eggs to main courses. Salsas can be made from fresh, raw vegetables or cooked. Every Mexican food chef has his/her particular way of making salsa. It's very personal and always unique. Basic ingredients are chilies, tomatoes, onions, cilantro, and spices.

Tacos
There are two types of tacos: fried and soft; traditionally made with corn tortillas – although today some restaurants use small flour tortillas. Deep-fried and lightly fried tacos are folded in half and stuffed with either shredded beef or chicken – and topped with lettuce, tomatoes, cheese, and a little Salsa Fresca.

Soft tacos are not fried. The tortillas are warmed and traditionally stuffed, with either carne asada (grilled, marinated steak), carnitas (pork), or fried fish.

Tamales
These are made from masa dough filled with meat, vegetables, and spices (or fruit) and wrapped in a corn husk (or banana leaf), and steamed until hot.

Tequila
This is the national drink of Mexico. First created by the Mayans in the form of pulque, a less potent drink made from the agave cactus. When the Spaniards arrived in Mexico, they drank the pulque with pleasure. After much experimenting with different types of agave, tequila was invented, which is made from blue agave and is about 80 proof.

Tomatillos
These look like tiny green tomatoes. but they are a relative of the gooseberry family. They're flavorful and used in many sauces, particularly salsa verde (green sauce}.

Tortas
Mexican sandwiches made from a hard Mexican roll (bolillo) cut in half and layered inside with tomatoes, avocados or guacamole and carne asada, shredded beef or chicken, cheese, and salsa.

Tostadas
Similar to fried tacos, but they are served a fried flat corn tortilla topped with a layer of beans, shredded beef or chicken, lettuce, tomatoes, cheese, avocado, and salsa.

TYPES OF CHILIES

There are over 60 varieties of chilies, chili peppers, or hot peppers, ranging from very mild to fiery hot. Chilies are a key ingredient in most Mexican food dishes. The heat in chilies comes from the oils concentrated in their seeds and membranes. The heat of a chili lasts six minutes before it dissipates, which can be a long time if your mouth, eyes, or skin are burning.

Ancho
Dried dark red poblano chilies. They're mildly flavored and used in many sauces.

Chipotles
Made from jalapenos that have been dried and smoked. They are sold both dried and canned in adobo, or a rich, smoky, dark reddish-brown sauce. Their flavor is uniquely delicious.

Chilacas
Look and taste much like the green chilies – California and Guyon chilies. They are mild.

Chile de Arbol
Also known as the Cola de Rata. It's about the size of your little finger. These are often dried, toasted, and used to decorate Mexican food dishes.

Cola de Rata
Also known as Rat-tail Chile and as the Chile de Arbol. It's about the size of your little finger. These are often dried, toasted, and used as a garnish.

Green or California
They are light green, mild, medium-sized, and tapered at the end.

Guajillo
A dried red chili that gives more color than taste to Mexican food recipes. It's about four to five inches long, narrow, and has smooth skin.

Guero of Gueritos
Small, yellow, and tapered on the end. They're sold either fresh or pickled and are medium-hot.

Jalapeno
The most recognizable and widely used of all Mexican chilies. Rarely do you see a Mexican table without a small bowl of jalapenos from a can, pickled in escabeche with carrots and onions. They are plump, about an inch or two in length, medium to dark green, and fairly hot. They're used as a condiment, in salsa and other dishes.

Habanero

The hottest chilies in the world! Bright orange and looking like tiny bell peppers, their flavor is delicious, if used sparingly. They are used widely throughout southern Mexico, particularly the Yucatan. Originally discovered by the Mayans, they are said to have mystical healing powers and to impart a great sense of well-being.

Mulato

Frequently used when ancho chilies are called for in a recipe. It's deep brown, longer and more tapered than the ancho, and is a bit more pungent.

Pasilla

Seven inches long and very thin. They're dark green like the ancho but have more fire to them.

Pequin

Tiny, dried red bullets of fiery heat. They add a unique flavor to many dishes. To use, crumble the dried pod between your thumb and forefinger. Piquin peppers are also called CHILITEPINS OR CHILTEPIN PEPPERS, tiny seedy red peppers used for seasoning in salsas in combinations with other chilies. They are also used in pickling. They are very, very hot!

Poblanos

Used in Chili Rellenos. They are dark green and about the size of bell pepper, but tapered at one end. They can be mild or quite hot. They're best fresh, but also available in cans.

Serrano

HOT! They're about an inch and a half long and bright green and used frequently in salsas. They're best fresh, but also available in cans.

APPETIZERS AND SALSA

Ceviche

This light and refreshing dish can be served as an appetizer or side dish for lunch or brunch. I first discovered ceviche when. I was working in Houston, TX, and finally realized I could make it myself. The main secret to success is to use very fresh fish.

INGREDIENTS

1½ pounds fresh sea bass or flounder deboned and cut into ½" pieces.

(Any fish or shellfish will work. Scallops and shrimp are especially good.)

7 whole fresh limes *(enough Juice to cover fish)*

3 medium tomatoes, seeds removed and diced

1 small red onion, sliced very thin and cut into small pieces

1 whole avocado, ripe, but firm, cut into ½ cubes

1 tablespoon fresh cilantro, finely chopped

¼ cup fresh oregano, finely chopped

(OR - substitute 2 teaspoons dried)

1 teaspoon salt

¼ teaspoon freshly ground black pepper

Lime wedges and avocado slices for garnish

DIRECTIONS

- Dice the fish, approximately ½" cubes. *(If using shrimp be sure to use cleaned, de-veined, and steamed or parboiled shrimp.)*

- Spread out fish *(except shrimp)* in a non-metallic bowl. Squeeze the juice of 6 limes and pour over the mixed seafood to cover it completely – use more limes if necessary.

- Cover the dish with plastic wrap and refrigerate **overnight**. *(This step cooks the fish, do not marinate shrimp, they tend to get tough).*

An hour or two before serving:

- Chop and dice the tomatoes, onions, avocado, and herbs.

- Drain the marinated seafood in a colander to remove excess lime juice and pat dry with paper towels and place in a mixing bowl.

- Add shrimp, vegetables, and seasonings to the marinated seafood.

- Squeeze the juice of one lime and sprinkle over the mixture and toss well.

- Refrigerate until ready to serve.

- When ready to serve, arrange in individual serving bowls.

- Garnish with lime and avocado slices.

Servings: *Varies*
Cooking Time (in lime juice): 8 hours

RECIPE TIPS

- You can alter the recipe to suit your own taste. Make it as spicy or as mild as you wish.

- Do not marinate shrimp, it will get tough. Steam or parboil the shrimp and add them to the mix a few hours before serving.

Chicken Sopes

Chicken sopes can be made from any salad ingredients that you happen to have in your refrigerator – add chicken, feta cheese, and refried beans, then served in handmade masa cups (sopes). This fun and tasty dish is so simple, it may become one of your favorites – tasty enough for a light brunch.

INGREDIENTS

2 cooked chicken breasts cut into small pieces

1½ cups refried beans

1 cup tomatoes, diced

1 large onion, finely diced *(red onion is best)*

3 ounces feta cheese

1 cup lettuce, finely shredded

Red or green hot sauce

1 pint sour cream *(For more traditional taste use Crema Mexicana)*

Cooking oil *(enough to fill small frying pan to ¾" full)*

1 to 2 large firm-ripe avocados, mashed with salt and pepper to taste

2 cups MASECA® Instant Corn Masa Flour *(Can also use Quaker or Red Mill)*

¼ teaspoon salt

1¼ cups water

DIRECTIONS

PREPARE THE FILLING

- Cut up the chicken into small bite-sized pieces and chop the vegetables – refrigerate until ready.

MAKE THE SOPES

- In a medium bowl, mix masa harina, salt and water thoroughly (easiest to do with your hands) for about 2 minutes to form a soft dough. If the dough feels dry, add more water (one tablespoon at a time).

- Divide masa into 20 portions and roll into balls, cover with plastic wrap to prevent drying.

- Place a ball between two sheets of heavy-duty plastic wrap. Roll out or flatten the ball to form a 2½" to 3" diameter circle, about 3/8" thick (this is your sope).

- Cook each sope for one minute on a very hot griddle. Turn and cook the 2nd side until lightly browned.

- Carefully remove from heat. On one side, pinch the edges to form a rim about ¼" high. The sopes will be hot! Be careful not to burn yourself.

- Set aside and keep covered with a cloth napkin.

ASSEMBLE THE SOPES
- Place beans in a pan over low heat, stirring occasionally.

- Heat a ¼ layer of oil in a heavy frying pan - fry the sopes in hot oil until light golden brown - drain on paper towel.

- Spread one tablespoon of heated beans on each sope.

- Top with chicken, tomato, onion, feta cheese, lettuce, sour cream, and avocado.

- Serve with your favorite taco (or hot) sauce.

Yield: 16 – 20 Sopes

Chili Relleno Salsa

This tasty salsa can be used as a topping for both Chili Rellenos con Queso and Chili Relleno Casserole.

INGREDIENTS

¼ cup cooking oil

1 large clove garlic, crushed

1 cup onion, finely chopped

1 (#2½) can solid pack tomatoes, mashed

1 can *(4 ounces)* Ortega® chopped green chilies

1 teaspoon salt

DIRECTIONS

- Heat oil in a medium-large, heavy-duty frying pan over medium heat.

- Add garlic and onion, stirring continuously - reduce heat if necessary, do not overcook.

- When nicely browned, add tomatoes, chilies, and salt (to taste).

- Simmer uncovered for 30 minutes or until of good sauce consistency – stir often.

Servings: 6 – ½ cup each

RECIPE TIPS

It is easier to prepare the salsa well ahead of time - even the night before and heat before serving.

Guacamole

Guacamole, avocado dip, originated in Mexico. The name comes from two Aztec Nahuatl words - ahuacatl (avocado) and molli (sauce). It is a wonderful appetizer with chips or can be used as a topping on almost any Mexican dish from nachos, to tacos, to enchiladas.

INGREDIENTS

5 large firm-ripe avocados, mashed

2 green onions, finely chopped

1 whole lime – juice only

1 tomato, finely chopped *(optional)*

¼ cup cilantro, finely chopped

1 small clove garlic, minced

DIRECTIONS

- Cut avocados in half, remove the seed and scoop out the avocado from the peel.

- Mash the avocado with a fork and place it in a bowl large enough to hold all the ingredients.

- Add the chopped onion, cilantro, lime juice, salt, and mix thoroughly.

- Chili peppers (jalapenos) can be chopped very fine and added to the mix if you like it hot!

- Keep the tomatoes separate until ready to serve.

- Remember that much of this is done to taste because of the variability in the fresh ingredients.

- Start with suggested amounts in this recipe and adjust to your taste.

- Cover with plastic wrap directly on the surface of the guacamole to prevent oxidation from the air reaching it.

- Refrigerate until ready to serve.

- Just before serving, drain juice from the chopped tomatoes and add to the guacamole, if you choose to use them.

Servings: 4

RECIPE TIPS

For very quick guacamole just take a ¼ cup of salsa and mix it in with your mashed avocados.

You don't need to have tomatoes in your guacamole.

To extend a limited supply of avocados, add either sour cream or cottage cheese to your guacamole dip. Not traditional, but It tastes great.

The trick to perfect guacamole is using tasty, ripe avocados. Check for ripeness by gently pressing the end of the avocado. If there is no give, the avocado is not ripe and will not have a good flavor. If there is a little give, the avocado is ripe. If there is a lot of give, the avocado may be too ripe and not good. It is always wise to taste test the avocados before using them in guacamole.

BEVERAGES

Creamy Margaritas

You will love this interesting change up from the traditional margarita – it is a must try! This luscious combination of lime sherbet and evaporated milk will put a sparkle in your eyes and a smile on your lips with or without the alcohol.

INGREDIENTS

2 cups lime sherbet or sorbet

1 can (12 ounces) Nestle® CARNATION® Evaporated Milk

1 cup ice cubes

2 tablespoons *(1 shot)* tequila *(optional)*

Coarse salt *(optional)*

Fresh lime slices

DIRECTIONS

- Blend first four ingredients in electric blender until smooth.

- If desired, dip rims of margarita glasses into water, then in salt and shake off excess.

- Pour margarita mixture into glasses.

- Garnish with lime slices.

Horchata

Horchata is a traditional Latin beverage that is served in most Latin American countries and any good Mexican Restaurant in the U.S. It is a combination of a unique flavor and texture. It is often served with meals or as a nutritious snack.

INGREDIENTS

2 cups white rice, rinsed, drained

1 cinnamon stick, broken in half

4 cups boiling water

2/3 cup granulated sugar

1½ cups whole milk

(Traditionally evaporated milk is used and a good quality brand can be substituted)

1 cup ice water (without the ice)

Ice cubes

Ground cinnamon for sprinkling

Lime slices for garnish *(optional)*

DIRECTIONS

- Combine rice, cinnamon stick, and boiling water in a large bowl, cool.

- Cover with plastic wrap and refrigerate overnight.

TO SERVE
- Remove cinnamon stick, drain (reserve soaking water), and spoon rice into a blender.

- Blend on high for 3 – 4 minutes until mixture is very smooth.

- Add the reserved soaking water and sugar.

- Blend for an additional 2 minutes.

- Strain mixture through a cheesecloth or fine sieve into a pitcher, pressing the rice solids until only a dry paste remains – discard paste.

- Add milk and cold water.

- Taste and add a little more sugar to taste.

- Cover and refrigerate until ready to serve – minimum of two hours.

- Stir well before serving.

- Pour into tall glasses with ice cubes.

- Sprinkle with cinnamon, garnish with lime slices.

Servings: 6

Mexican Coffee

In Mexico, they love their coffee hot, strong, sweet, and with a touch of spice. This coffee will be a nice change of pace from your usual morning coffee or fun to serve to friends when they come to chat.

INGREDIENTS

 4 cups espresso-style coffee (very hot)

 ¾ cups half-and-half, warmed slightly

 3 tablespoons light brown sugar, packed

 2 tablespoons unsweetened cocoa

DIRECTIONS

- Make espresso coffee *(use immediately while very hot).*

- Combine coffee, half-and-half *(slightly warmed),* brown sugar, cocoa, and cinnamon in a blender and blend 1 minute on high. *(Be careful hot coffee expands when blended and can end up all over the counter.)*

- Pour into warmed mugs.

- Top with lightly sweetened whipped cream and a sprinkle of cinnamon or chocolate shavings. *(**Note:** For special occasions, serve with chocolate-dipped cinnamon sticks for stirring.)*

Servings: 4

Mexican Hot Chocolate

There are endless versions of Mexican Hot Chocolate – below are three of them. This comforting drink is enjoyed at breakfast, a late supper, and on holidays and special occasions. It is usually served with either sweet bread or basic white bread which they dunk into the hot liquid – YUM!

BASIC MEXICAN HOT CHOCOLATE

INGREDIENTS

2 ½ Cups of milk

1 (3 oz.) Mexican Chocolate Tablet like Abuelita (Nestle's) or Ibarra cut into pieces

DIRECTIONS

- Place chopped chocolate and milk in a medium-sized saucepan and simmer for a few minutes over low heat, stirring constantly until chocolate is completely dissolved.

- Remove from the heat and use an immersion mixer to form a nice foam. You can also use a blender (loosely covered) to form the foam. BE CAREFUL – blend small amounts at a time, *hot liquids tend to explode in a blender*.

- Serve and enjoy!

HOMEMADE MEXICAN CHOCOLATE MIX

INGREDIENTS

2 cups of cold milk

3 Tablespoons cocoa powder

1½ tablespoon of ground almonds

1½ tablespoon of ground pecans

¼ teaspoon of ground cinnamon

½ teaspoon of vanilla extract

1½ tablespoons of sugar (more to taste)

DIRECTIONS

- Grind the pecans, almonds, and cinnamon into a fine meal using a spice grinder. If you don't have a spice grinder, try a blender. Another option is to buy almond meal and skip the pecans.

- Place dry ingredients – (ground pecans, almonds, cinnamon), cocoa powder, and sugar in a small bowl and mix well.

- Once you have your dry mix, place in a small saucepan with the cold milk and vanilla. Mix thoroughly with the cold milk to avoid forming any clumps, this is very important since the almond and pecans will slightly thicken the mix.

- Serve and enjoy!

RECIPE TIPS

There will always be solids that settle to the bottom, no matter how much you blend the ingredients. Serve with a stick of cinnamon to stir the drink as it's enjoyed.

The chocolate package says 4 cups of milk for each 3 oz. tablet but the flavor too light for me – find your preference.

Use roasted or toasted almonds if possible. If you don't have pecans, using only almonds is fine.

Use high-quality cocoa powder – it makes a huge difference in taste. Experiment with the ingredients until you find your favorite mix.

SPICEY MEXICAN HOT CHOCOLATE*** (My Preference)

This recipe is made with cocoa powder, cinnamon, vanilla, and a mix of chili powders for just a touch of warmth. It has just the right amount of chocolate and spice.

INGREDIENTS

3 cups milk *(2% is fine if you're watching calories, but whole milk is better for a rich hot chocolate)*

3 tablespoons granulated sugar

2 tablespoons unsweetened cocoa powder

½ teaspoon ground cinnamon

½ teaspoon vanilla extract

¼ teaspoon ancho chili powder (this is the best choice)

Pinch of cayenne powder or more as desired

Pinch of salt

2 ounces unsweetened chocolate (for authenticity use Abuelita (Nestle's) or Ibarra)

DIRECTIONS

- Add the milk, sugar, cocoa powder, cinnamon, vanilla, chili powder, and salt to a pot.

- Stirring constantly, bring it to medium heat, and add the chocolate.

- Whisk until the chocolate is melted and thoroughly blended, ~ 5 minutes. The chocolate should be hot, but not boiling.

- Serve in warm mugs and top with whipped cream and chocolate shavings, with cinnamon sticks for stirring.

Servings: 4 small cups

RECIPE TIPS

Add more sugar as desired for sweetness, and more cayenne powder to your preferred heat level.

MAIN DISHES

Chicken Tortilla Casserole

If you want a delicious Mexican-flavored main dish that can be put together easily, this is it!

INGREDIENTS

4 skinless, boneless chicken breast halves (4 ounces each)

8 ounces sharp cheddar cheese, grated

1 package fresh corn tortillas (12)

2 cans (4 ounces) Ortega® chopped green chilies

1 can cream of chicken soup

1 can cream of mushroom soup

1½ cups half-and-half

DIRECTIONS

- Season chicken breast halves with salt and pepper, wrap in foil.

- Bake for 1 hour and 15 minutes at 350° F.

- Save juice - Cut chicken into bite-sized pieces.

- Mix diced chilies, both soups, and half-and-half in a large bowl.

- Add chicken pieces to the mix.

- Divide tortillas into two stacks and cut them into 1" pieces.

- Place the following in a large, buttered casserole dish - in layers.

- Juice from baked chicken.

- Pieces of 6 corn tortillas.

- Spread half the mixture on top of the tortillas.

- Sprinkle half the grated cheese as the next layer.

- Layer with remaining pieces of 6 corn tortillas.

- Cover with remaining mixture.

- Top with the remaining half of cheese.

- Cover and refrigerate for 24 hours.

- Bake for 1 hour at 300° F. *(Sometimes it takes a little longer)*.

Servings: 6 – 8

RECIPE TIPS

This is an easy meal with a fairly long prep time because of the baking time for the chicken, but an excellent choice for a meal that can be prepared the day before and served on an evening when someone else in the family needs to pop the meal into the oven for you. Or it can be prepared on Saturday for a leisurely Sunday dinner.

You can also buy a roasted chicken from the supermarket, which cuts your prep time down to the bare minimum.

Chilaquiles

This homey Mexican dish is usually served for breakfast, and it also makes an excellent dinner entrée. This is a simplified version of the original which was made with fried tortilla strips. It is incredibly easy and tasty.

INGREDIENTS

2 large boneless skinless chicken breasts

2 cups chicken broth

2 cups enchilada sauce *(red or green)*

(Good brands: El Paso or Las Palmas)

6 cups tortilla chips *(regular, not flavored)*

10 large eggs

1 cup milk

1½ cups Mexican Style cheese, shredded

1 can Ortega® jalapenos

1 small to medium red or white onion, chopped

2 tablespoons vegetable oil *(or cooking spray)*

1 teaspoon salt

Sour cream for topping *(optional)*

1 whole firm-ripe avocado peeled and mashed with salt and pepper to taste

DIRECTIONS

- In a large cooking pan, add ½ cup enchilada sauce, 2 cups chicken broth, and stir.

- Boil the chicken breasts until cooked through ~ 30 minutes.

- Remove the chicken from the sauce and shred with a fork or break into small pieces.

- Set chicken aside

- Preheat the oven to 400° F.

- Whisk eggs and milk together, add cheese.

- In a pan large enough to hold all the ingredients, sauté onion in oil.

- Add salt and jalapenos *(optional)*.

- Cook and stir for a few minutes.

- Add the egg mixture and thicken for about one minute.

- In a large bag, add chips and remaining enchilada sauce.

- Shake until sauce has coated the chips.

- Immediately add chips to the egg mixture and stir until eggs have coated the chips. *(The eggs will be a bit runny.)*

- Mix in the shredded chicken.

- Pour into greased casserole pan (9" X13") and top with remaining cheese and additional sauce.

- Bake for 10 minutes to finish cooking the eggs and melt the cheese.

- Serve immediately.

Servings: 6

RECIPE TIPS

Serve with bowls of chopped fresh cilantro, hot enchilada sauce, avocado, and sour cream as toppings.

If you would like to try the original style, cut tortillas into 1" strips (which is the way the chef in Salt Lake did it). Heat the oil in a skillet until hot. Lightly brown the strips and drain them on paper towels. Use in place of tortilla chips. The tortilla chips make up the "quick" version.

The recipe can easily be cut in half – use an 8" X 8" baking dish.

Chili Relleno Casserole

This is a family favorite variation on the more traditional Chili Rellenos con Queso. It can be prepared the night before and popped into the oven when you get home from work. It is great for a busy weeknight and delicious enough for guests.

INGREDIENTS

4 cans (4 ounces) Ortega® Whole Green Chilies

1 pound sharp cheddar cheese, grated

1 pound Monterey Jack cheese, grated

4 large eggs, lightly beaten

2 cups milk

½ cup flour

1 teaspoon salt

DIRECTIONS

- Preheat the oven to 350° F.

- Cut chilies into 2" strips and remove seeds.

- Place half of the chili strips on the bottom of a buttered 9" X13" casserole dish - evenly spaced.

- Combine the two kinds of cheese and spread over the chilies.

- Top with remaining chili strips - evenly spaced.

- Stir lightly beaten eggs, milk, flour, and salt - just until mixed - do not beat.

- Pour mixture over layered chilies and cheese.

- Bake 45-50 minutes. *(Be sure center is set.)*

- Cut into squares and serve with **Chili Relleno Salsa**.

Servings: 6 (Can be slightly more or less depending on serving size)

RECIPE TIPS

Can be prepared the night before and refrigerated overnight, which may extend the cooking time slightly. Be sure that the center is set before removing from the oven.

Chili Rellenos con Queso

Chili Rellenos are a traditional Mexican dish that has many variations. This is an excellent version given to me by a dear friend that will be a hit with both family and guests.

INGREDIENTS

3 cans (8 ounces) Ortega® Whole Green Chilies

1½ cups sharp cheddar cheese, grated

6 large egg whites

3 tablespoons flour

1 dash salt

6 large egg yolks

Salad oil or shortening

1 recipe **Chili Relleno Salsa**

DIRECTIONS

- Slit each pepper and remove seeds.

- Stuff with cheese and roll in flour - set aside.

- Beat egg whites until stiff- but not dry. *(Peaks should form easily.)*

- Add flour and salt to egg yolks. Beat until lemon-colored and thick.

- Gently fold yolk mixture into egg whites *(DO NOT beat)*.

- Heat oil in a heavy-duty hot frying pan to 375° F.

- Spoon ½ cup+ of egg batter into hot oil and spread into an egg-shaped form.

- Create two to three mounds in the pan. *(Allow room for easy turning - don't crowd.)*

- As batter begins to set, gently top each mound with a cheese-stuffed pepper.

- Immediately cover each chili with more batter.

- Continue cooking until the underside is nicely browned - adjust oil temp as needed.

- Turn carefully and brown the second side.

- Remove from pan and place on paper towels to absorb oil.

- Serve at once with warm **Chili Relleno Salsa.**

Servings: 6

Drunken Chicken with Apples and Almonds

This recipe has a delicious sweet and sour flavor with tequila being the magic ingredient. Serve it with green or steamed white rice and flour tortillas to soak up the sauce.

INGREDIENTS

¾ cup raisins

½ cup sherry

1 cup flour

½ teaspoon salt

½ teaspoon black pepper

8 skinless chicken thighs, bone-in

1 whole white onion, peeled, halved, and thinly sliced

3 large cloves garlic, mashed

2 whole Granny Smith apples, peeled, cored, and finely diced

1 cup slivered almonds

1 ripe plantain, peeled and sliced

1½ cups richly-flavored chicken stock

1 cup tequila

Chopped fresh cilantro, to garnish

DIRECTIONS

- Combine raisins and sherry in a small bowl, set aside so raisins can plump-up.

- Mix flour, salt, and pepper in a large plastic bag.

- Heat oil in a large frying pan.

- Shake each thigh in seasoned flour and place in the frying pan.

- Cook, turning as needed until all sides are nicely browned.

- Drain on paper towels and cover.

- Heat the remaining vegetable oil in a different deep frying pan.

- Add the onion slices and crushed garlic - cook for 2 to 3 minutes.

- Peel, core and dice the apples and add to onion/garlic mix with the almonds and plantain slices.

- Cook, stirring occasionally, for 3 to 4 minutes.

- Then add the raisins and sherry mixture.

- Place chicken pieces in the pan and pour the stock and tequila over the chicken.

- Cover the pan with a tight-fitting lid and cook for 15 minutes.

- Remove the lid and cook for 10 minutes more, or until the sauce has reduced by about half.

- Test chicken thighs to see if they are tender by lifting one out of the pan and piercing it in the thickest part with a sharp knife or skewer. *(If the juices come out clear, it is ready. If not, cook a little longer, when ready, remove from stove.)*

- Serve in a large bowl, sprinkled with fresh cilantro or other fresh herbs.

Servings: 6

Enchiladas Rojas de Queso

*The sauce is very close to the recipe given to me years ago in California by Alicia, who owned a small Mexican restaurant very near our home. You can also fill the enchiladas with chicken (see **Spicy Chicken Enchiladas Verdes** for chicken preparation).*

INGREDIENTS

THE ENCHILADAS

4 cups Queso Fresco (Mexican Cheese), crumbled

(OR - Monterey Jack cheese shredded)

1 dozen 6" corn tortillas

1 bunch green onions, chopped

Fresh cilantro, chopped

1 pint sour cream

1 or 2 large avocados, mashed and seasoned with salt and pepper

THE SAUCE

3 tablespoons lard

(Lard is traditional and adds unique flavor - vegetable oil can be substituted)

3 tablespoons flour

¼ cup chili powder

2 cups chicken stock

1 can (10 ounces) tomato paste

2 large cloves garlic, minced

1 teaspoon dried oregano

1 teaspoon ground cumin

½ teaspoon salt

THE GARNISH

2 bunches of green onions

1 small bunch of fresh cilantro

DIRECTIONS

MAKE THE SAUCE

- In a medium-sized saucepan, heat oil, add flour, smoothing and stirring with a wooden spoon.

- Cook for 1 minute – until mixture is bubbling well.

- Add chili powder and cook for 30 seconds more.

- Add stock, tomato paste, garlic, oregano, and cumin - Stir with a wire whisk to combine.

- Bring to a boil, reduce heat to low, and cook for 15 minutes.

- The sauce will thicken and smooth out.

- Adjust the seasonings.

MAKE THE ENCHILADAS

- Heat ½" cooking oil in a small (6 inch) skillet over moderately high heat to 375° F.

- Add the tortillas one at a time turning over almost immediately. They may puff but should not stiffen at all. *(Tortillas should be warm, soft, and flexible.)*

- Lay tortillas on paper towels and set aside.

- Place 1 cup of sauce on the bottom of a 13" x 9" baking dish.

- Dip a tortilla into the remaining sauce in the cooking pan and transfer to a plate.

- Spread ¼ cup cheese down the center of the tortilla and roll up tightly.

- Repeat process with remaining tortillas.

- Transfer enchiladas to baking dish, seam side down.

- Pour the remaining sauce over the enchiladas, followed by the remaining cheese.

- Cover with foil and bake for 20 minutes.

- Garnish with a large stripe of sour cream, chopped green onions, and cilantro – serve immediately.

- Provide a small side dish of **Guacamole** for additional topping.

Servings: 4

Green Chili Verde (Arizona Style)

Green Chili Verde (Stew) is an excellent cold winter's night dish. The recipe is easy to double for large groups. Can be made ahead of time and reheated.

INGREDIENTS

2-pound pork roast cut in 1-inch cubes

4 cans (4 ounces) Ortega® chopped green chilies

2 large cloves garlic, finely chopped

3 large onions, finely chopped

¼ cup fresh Jalapeno chilies, stemmed, seeded, and finely diced

(You may prefer 1 to 2 tablespoons for a milder dish)

(Ortega® canned Jalapenos can be substituted for the fresh chilies)

¼ cup fresh cilantro, chopped finely *(add more to taste)*

1 can (#2½) whole tomatoes, crushed

1 can chicken broth

2 cubes chicken bullion

1 cup water

Salt and black pepper to taste

DIRECTIONS

- Fry pork cubes until nicely browned in a heavy cooking pot - use a small amount of oil.

- Season with salt and pepper *(adjust later to taste)*.

- Add all other ingredients and stir well.

- Bring to boil; then, reduce heat, cover, and simmer for 4 hours or until pork is tender.

- Add small equal portions of water and chicken broth as needed to keep pork well-covered.

- Last 30 minutes to 1 hour, remove the lid, and cook down until thick.

- Keep the heat low and stir occasionally until the mixture reaches desired consistency.

- Serve immediately with warm flour tortillas.

Servings: 4

RECIPE TIPS

Hot or Mild? You may want to try it on the mild side the first time and then add a few more jalapenos each time you make it until you get it just right.

Homemade Tacos

These tacos take a lot of work but are worth every minute. Be sure to enlist some helpers! Once the tacos are ready to serve, it becomes a fun build-it-yourself dinner. This recipe was given to me by my boyfriend's mom when I was 19-years-old. I have tweaked it a little over the years, but it is still the best homemade taco recipe around.

INGREDIENTS

2 pounds lean ground beef

2 tablespoons chili powder *(adjust to taste)*

1 teaspoon cayenne pepper *(adjust to taste)*

1½ teaspoon salt

½ teaspoon freshly ground black pepper

2 dozen fresh corn tortillas

½ head iceberg lettuce, shredded

4 medium-large tomatoes, diced

1 pound cheddar cheese, grated *(for creamier taste, use Velveeta)*

1 pint sour cream

2 large firm-ripe well-mashed avocados *(Haas preferred)*

Taco sauce *(bottled – Macayo® is a good one)*

DIRECTIONS

PREPARE INGREDIENTS

- Shred lettuce, place in a large bowl, cover with a damp paper towel and refrigerate.

- Chop tomatoes and onions, placing each in a small serving bowl, cover, and refrigerate.

- Mash avocados, add salt and pepper to taste, cover and refrigerate.

- Grate cheese and refrigerate.

- Fry hamburger in large heavy skillet until brown and crumbled - use small amount oil on medium-high heat, stir frequently.

51

- Add salt and pepper while cooking.

- When fully browned and crumbled, add chili powder, cayenne pepper - mix well.

- Add additional chili powder and cayenne to taste.

- Drain all excess grease and set mixture aside *(ok to leave in frying pan)*.

PREPARE FOR COOKING AND ASSEMBLING TACOS

- Preheat the oven to 250° F.

- Place a double paper towel on the bottom of 2 or 3 baking dishes (13" X 9").

- Place a double paper towel on a large plate.

- Begin heating vegetable or Wesson Oil to HOT - in a small 6" to 8" frying pan.

- Set up an assembly line - have your helper in place.

- Right-handed people will probably work from left to right *(tortillas, frying pan, large plate with paper towel, hamburger, cheese, baking dishes with paper towels)*.

COOK THE TORTILLAS

- Place the first tortilla into hot oil, cook until it begins to bubble slightly.

- Turn over carefully with long-handled tongs and cook for a few seconds more.

- Lift one side of the tortilla with tongs to a right angle with the bottom of the frying pan - let it cook for a few seconds until the tortilla holds the shape.

- Turn it over and place the right-angled piece in oil and cook for a few seconds longer.

- Remove tortilla from oil and place on a large plate with a paper towel to absorb excess oil and cool slightly.

- DO NOT overcook. Tortillas should be lightly crisp, but still pliable. Repeat the process!

- As the cook continues to cook tortillas - the helper should begin to assemble the tacos.

ASSEMBLE THE TACOS

- Add 1 to 2 tablespoons of hamburger mixture *(don't overfill)* and top with cheese.

- Place in the baking dish with paper towels on the bottom. *(When the dish is full, place it in the oven and start filling the second baking dish.)*

- By the time the cooking is complete, the first baking dish will be ready!

- SERVE with lettuce, tomatoes, onions, sour cream, avocados, taco sauce.

Servings: 8 (Adult males usually eat 4-5, women and children 2-3)

RECIPE TIPS

Preparation time is approximate. It will go be much easier and go faster if you have help. You need one person to cook the taco shells and a helper to add the meat and cheese.

(American) Indian Tostadas

My mom taught me how to make fry bread when I was in high school. I loved it then and still love it today. I learned later at the Arizona State Fair that you can use it instead of tortillas to make great tostadas. This meal-in-itself is served in many places throughout Arizona including the cafe in Supai at the bottom of the Grand Canyon. It is a delicious blend of two cultures.

INGREDIENTS

1 recipe **Navajo Fry Bread**

3 cups refried beans – warm

Lettuce, shredded

Tomatoes, diced

Green onions, chopped

Cheddar cheese, grated

1 pint sour cream

2 large firm-ripe well-mashed avocados *(Haas preferred)*

Taco sauce *(bottled – Macayo® is a good one)*

DIRECTIONS

- Make 1 recipe of ***Navajo Fry Bread.***

- *(Can be made in advance and warmed.)*

- Heat refried beans.

- Spread each piece of fry bread with ½ cup refried beans.

- From here it is a build-it-yourself.

- Serve lettuce, tomato, green onion, cheese, avocado, sour cream, and taco sauce.

Servings: 6

Spicy Enchiladas Verdes

These enchiladas have a tangy flavor with a great kick from the spicy sauce. With plenty of spicy flavor from the Serrano chilies and lots of contrasting flavor from the cilantro, onion, and creamy tasting Queso Fresco, it is delectable, indeed!

INGREDIENTS

2 cooked chicken breasts, deboned and shredded

6 fresh Serrano chilies, stems removed *(adjust to taste)*

1 pound tomatillos, husked, stemmed, and halved

1 small white onion, finely chopped

2 large cloves garlic, minced

1½ teaspoon ground cumin

¼ cup vegetable oil

1½ cubes chicken bouillon

Water as needed

16 corn tortillas (6")

¼ cup vegetable oil

1 cup crumbled Queso Fresco (Mexican Cheese)

(Increase to 2 Cups for cheese enchiladas)

Fresh cilantro, chopped

Salt and black pepper to taste

Sour cream and mashed avocado for toppings *(optional)*

DIRECTIONS

- Place the trimmed tomatillos and chilies in a pot with just enough water to cover and bring to a boil; cook until the tomatillos turn a dull green, remove from heat, and strain off the liquid.

- Place the tomatillos, chilies, ¼ of the onion, garlic, ground cumin, a little salt, and enough water to cover the vegetables in a blender or food processor and blend until smooth. *(Should be liquefied.)*

- Heat ¼ cup vegetable oil in a heavy-duty skillet until just warm (about 30 seconds), and pour the blended chili mixture into the oil and bring to a boil.

- Immediately stir in chicken bouillon cubes and 1 sprig of cilantro.

- Reduce the heat to medium-low and simmer sauce for 25-30 minutes, stirring occasionally.

- When cooking is complete, remove the cilantro and reduce heat to very low, just to keep warm and continue with the next step.

- In another pan, heat the oil and fry the tortillas briefly, using tongs to handle.

- After frying, give each tortilla a dip in the salsa and lay out on plates, filling each with a little shredded chicken *(do not overfill)* and a tablespoon of salsa verde.

- Roll up the tortillas and top with more salsa, crumbled Queso Fresco, remaining diced onion, and chopped cilantro.

- Serve hot with bowls of sour cream and mashed avocado provided for toppings.

- Enjoy! They will disappear quickly.

Servings: 4

RECIPE TIPS

For cheese enchiladas, eliminate the chicken and fill fried tortillas that have been dipped into the sauce with 2 teaspoons of shredded Queso Fresco cheese.

Be careful not to fill the enchiladas too full of either chicken or cheese, they should be thin.

You may want to find a good Mexican grocery store to purchase the tomatillos and the fresh jalapenos.

Tamale Pie

Tamale Pie is one of those quintessential American budget-friendly, pot-luck casserole dishes with Mexican influence. It was probably invented by someone who had a taste of real tamales and tried to recreate the flavor in a cornbread casserole. This one may turn out to be a favorite of kids in the family.

INGREDIENTS

1½ pound ground beef

2 tablespoons cooking oil (or cooking spray)

2 small onions, finely chopped

1 large green bell pepper, finely chopped

3 medium to large cloves garlic, minced

1 teaspoon salt

2 tablespoons chili powder

1 dash black pepper

1 can (15 ounces) tomato sauce

1 can (28 ounces) whole tomatoes, crushed

1 can (4 ounces) ripe coarsely cut black olives *(optional)*

CORNMEAL TOPPING

¾ cup yellow cornmeal

2 cups cold water

½ teaspoon salt

½ teaspoon chili powder

1 tablespoon butter *(no substitutes)*

½ cup cheddar or Mexican blend cheese for topping *(optional)*

DIRECTIONS

- Preheat the oven to 375° F.

- Brown ground beef in hot oil.

- Add onions, garlic, and green pepper – cook until vegetables are soft and slightly browned.

- Add 1 teaspoon salt, 2 tablespoons chili powder, pepper, tomato sauce, crushed tomatoes, and olives.

- Heat to boiling; reduce heat and simmer on low heat, uncovered, for 45 -50 minutes, or until thickened, stir occasionally.

- Set filling aside.

- In a saucepan, combine cornmeal, water, salt, and chili powder.

- Cook over medium heat, stirring constantly, until thick - stir in butter.

- Spread half of the cornmeal mixture into a buttered 9" X 13" baking dish.

- Spoon filling over bottom crust; spoon remaining cornmeal mixture on top of casserole.

- Bake for 45 minutes. If desired, sprinkle ½ cup cheese over the crust about 5 minutes before casserole is done.

Servings: 6

DESSERTS

Cheesecake Mexicana

The flavor of Mexico in a traditional American dessert.

INGREDIENTS

CRUST

½ cup chocolate wafer crumbs

1/3 cup butter, melted

1 tablespoon sugar

¼ teaspoon cinnamon

FILLING

4 packages *(8 ounces)* cream cheese, softened

1½ cup sugar

4 large eggs

1 cup sour cream

¼ cup coffee-flavored liqueur

1 teaspoon vanilla extract

1 cup whipping cream

1 cup semisweet chocolate chips, melted

½ teaspoon cinnamon

Sweetened whipped cream and shaved dark chocolate candy for garnish

DIRECTIONS

MAKE THE CRUST

- Combine wafer crumbs, melted butter, 1 tablespoon sugar, and 1/3 teaspoon cinnamon in a small bowl.

- Press mixture evenly over the bottom of a buttered square 9" spring-form pan or very large glass pie plate for deep-dish pie. Refrigerate.

MAKE THE FILLING

- Beat cream cheese until smooth with electric beaters and gradually beat in 1½ cups sugar.

- Add eggs, one at a time, beating well.

- Stir in sour cream, liqueur, vanilla, whipping cream, melted chocolate, and ½ teaspoon cinnamon - blend well.

- Pour into the crust-lined pan and bake at 325° F. for 1 hour and 15 minutes.

- Do not open the oven door.

- Turn the oven off and leave cheesecake in the oven for another hour.

- Remove and cool slightly, then refrigerate overnight before serving.

- Serve with sweetened whipped cream, and sprinkled lightly with cinnamon and a few pieces of shaved dark chocolate candy *(or drizzled with chocolate syrup as shown in the picture)*.

Servings: Makes 8 to 12 servings depending on the size

Flan

Flan is one of the most common traditional Mexican desserts, and one of my favorite all-time desserts. It is rich, creamy, full of calories, and wonderful!

INGREDIENTS

2 cups sugar

8 large eggs

2 cups milk

1 cup half-and-half or light cream

1 dash salt

1 teaspoon vanilla extract

DIRECTIONS

- Preheat the oven to 350° F.

- Place baking rack in the top third of the oven.

- Place 1 cup of sugar in a small, heavy-duty saucepan or skillet over medium-low heat,

- Stir constantly with wire whisk for 3 to 4 minutes or until sugar is dissolved and caramel-colored.

- Immediately pour the melted sugar into an 8-cup baking dish; quickly swirl around to coat the bottom and 1 or 2 inches up the sides of the dish *(9" round baking dish also works very well)*.

- Whisk the eggs together in a large bowl.

- Whisk in the milk, half-and-half, vanilla, and remaining cup of sugar.

- Strain through a sieve into the baking dish on top of the caramelized sugar.

- Place the dish in a large roasting pan and set it on the oven rack.

- Pour boiling water into the roasting pan until it is halfway up the sides of the baking dish holding the flan.

- Bake for 50 - 60 minutes or until the knife inserted near the center comes out clean.

- Remove flan from water.

- Cool on wire rack.

- Refrigerate overnight.

TO SERVE

- Run a small spatula around the edge of the pan.

- Invert serving plate over the pan and turn over; shake gently to release.

- There will be a fair amount of liquid, so choose a serving plate with a rim.

- Serve in slices and top with a dollop of fresh, sweetened whipped cream.

Servings: 8

Mexican Pecan Cake

This cake is a Mexican dessert with a French influence. In Mexico, it is traditionally served with boiled milk, but Americanized it is served with whipped cream. Be prepared for it to melt in your mouth.

INGREDIENTS

1 cup fresh pecans

½ cup butter, softened

½ cup light brown sugar

1 teaspoon vanilla extract

¾ cup flour

1 dash salt

4 large eggs, separated

Whipped cream

Honey and butter drizzle *(see below)*

DIRECTIONS

- Preheat the oven to 350° F.

- Butter an 8" round spring-form cake pan.

- Toast the pecans in a dry frying pan for 5 minutes, shaking frequently. *(Toasting is optional.)*

- Place in a blender or food processor and process until finely ground - place in a mixing bowl.

- With an electric hand mixer, cream butter and sugar together in a different mixing bowl.

- Mix in egg yolks and vanilla.

- Add flour to the ground nuts and mix thoroughly.

- In a large bowl *(be sure it is grease-free)* beat the egg whites with the salt until soft peaks form.

- Fold the egg whites into the butter mixture - then gently fold in the flour and nut mixture.

- Carefully spoon the entire mixture into the buttered cake pan.

- Bake for 30 minutes or until a toothpick inserted in the center comes out clean.

- Cool the cake in the pan for 5 minutes, then remove the sides of the pan and stand the cake on a wire rack until cool.

- Remove the cake from the bottom of the pan and place it on a serving platter.

HONEY/BUTTER DRIZZLE

- Melt the butter in a small pan.

- Add the honey and bring to a boil, stirring constantly.

- Lower the heat and simmer for 3 minutes.

- Pour the honey mixture onto the cake.

- Serve warm or cold - with whipped cream.

Servings: 10

Navajo Fry Bread

This is the traditional bread of the Navajo Indians. It can be eaten for breakfast or as a dessert the way I have presented it in this recipe. It has been included because it is often used in Arizona and New Mexico as an alternative to tortillas.

INGREDIENTS

2 cups flour

1 tablespoon baking powder

½ teaspoon salt *(adjust to taste)*

1 tablespoon lard or shortening

¾ cup milk *(a little extra may be needed if the dough is too dry)*

Shortening for frying *(can also use vegetable oil)*

Powdered sugar and honey - for topping

DIRECTIONS

- Stir all dry ingredients together.

- Cut in lard *(or shortening)* - or you can mix well with fingers.

- Add milk and mix with a fork.

- Knead lightly until smooth. *(Be careful - over-kneading makes fry bread heavy.)*

- Divide dough into 6 equal parts - form balls.

- Roll out each ball into 8" circles ¼" thick.

- In a cast-iron skillet, heat the vegetable oil to about 365° F.

- You can check the oil to see if it is hot enough by either dropping a small piece of dough in the hot oil and seeing if it begins to fry, or by dipping the end of a wooden spoon in and seeing if that bubbles.

- Oil should be about 1" deep in a large cast-iron skillet.

- Take the formed dough and gently place it into the oil, being careful not to splatter the hot oil.

- Press down on the dough as it fries so the top is submersed into the hot oil.

- Fry until brown, and then turn with tongs to fry the other side.

- Each side will take approximately 3 to 4 minutes to cook.

- Place the cooked Fry Bread on a paper towel to absorb excess oil.

- Sprinkle with powdered sugar or a light dripping of honey.

- Serve immediately while warm.

Servings: 8

RECIPE TIPS

Indian Fry Bread can be kept warm in a 200° F. oven for up to 1 hour.

They refrigerate well and can be reheated in a 350° F. for 15 seconds.

Fry bread can also be used in place of tortillas for delicious tostadas.

Tres Leches (Three Milk Cake)

This exceptional dessert takes a little extra effort, but it is worth it. The cake is very rich and serves a large number of people, making it perfect for a family gathering or a dinner with friends. It is originally Nicaraguan but has become a traditional Mexican dessert. My first taste was in Houston. YUM!

INGREDIENTS

THE CAKE

1 cup all-purpose flour

1½ teaspoon baking powder

½ teaspoon cream of tartar

1 cup white sugar

5 large eggs

½ teaspoon vanilla extract

1/3 cup whole milk

TRES LECHES SYRUP

1 cup sweetened condensed milk

1 can *(12 ounces)* evaporated milk

1 cup heavy cream

1 teaspoon vanilla extract

1 tablespoon light rum *(optional)*

DIRECTIONS

- Preheat the oven to 350° F.

- Generously butter a 13" X 9" baking dish.

- Separate eggs into two large mixing bowls.

MAKE THE CAKE

- Beat ¾ cup sugar and the egg yolks until light and fluffy, about 5 minutes.

- Fold in the milk, vanilla, flour, and baking powder.

- Beat the egg whites to soft peaks, adding the cream of tartar after 20 seconds.

- Gradually add the remaining ¼ cup sugar and continue beating until the whites are glossy and firm, but not dry.

- Gently fold the whites into the yolk mixture. Pour this batter into the buttered baking dish.

- Bake the cake until it feels firm and an inserted toothpick comes out clean, about 40 to 50 minutes.

- Let the cake cool completely on a wire rack.

- Unmold onto a large, deep platter. Pierce the cake all over with a fork. Be very careful, or the cake will tear.

TRES LECHES SYRUP

- Combine the evaporated milk, sweetened condensed milk, heavy cream, vanilla, and rum in a mixing bowl.

- Whisk until well blended.

- Pour the mixture over the cake, spooning the overflow back on top, until it is all absorbed. This requires a little patience.

- Refrigerate the cake for a minimum of two hours before serving.

MERINGUE

(Optional - This is used in some countries, but not all. It is a nice choice for a change. The cake is so rich that it can be served plain or with a little whipped cream and cinnamon for garnish.)

- Place ¾ cup plus 2 tablespoons sugar in a heavy saucepan with ¼ cup water.

- Cover and cook over high heat for 2 minutes.

- Uncover the pan and cook the sugar to the softball stage, 239° F. on a candy thermometer, 6 to 8 minutes.

- Meanwhile, beat the egg whites to soft peaks with the cream of tartar.

- Add 2 tablespoons of sugar and continue beating to stiff peaks.

- Pour the boiling sugar syrup in a thin stream into the stiff egg whites – beating continuously until the mixture is cool to the touch. *(The hot syrup "cooks" the egg whites.)*

- Using a wet spatula, frost the top and sides of the cake with a thick layer of meringue and refrigerate.

Servings: 10

ABOUT THE AUTHOR

Nancy N. Wilson is a writer, blogger, and bestselling author of more than 30 books – over half are cookbooks.

She was born and reared in a small farming community in Southern Arizona. She earned a B.S. Degree in Education and Psychology at Utah State University and an MBA at Thunderbird School of Global Management.

Her one constant lifetime companion has been cooking, which began as a young child when her mother gave her free rein in the kitchen to create masterpieces of flour, sugar, spices, and anything else she could find in the cupboards.

When she finally learned to follow a recipe, Mexican food and a wide variety of desserts (including cookies) were her two favorite types of foods to prepare.

Growing up in a small town in the 50s and 60s gave her many free hours to experiment and master the craft. She especially enjoyed cooking for her friends.

Even with college, marriage, and all the adventures of life, her love of cooking never faltered. She was always looking for new recipes and new creative touches for traditional dishes. She cooked her way through years of marriage, a divorce, and a multi-faceted career, and has achieved the status of "Best-Selling Cookbook Author."

She has lived and worked on both the East Coast and West Coast of the United States, consulted with major corporations in Europe and Japan, and traveled extensively throughout Central and South America.

In 2007, she returned to Arizona to live near her two sons and to do what she has always wanted to do – WRITE.

She now spends her time contributing to her "Healthy Living Blog, (https://Mamaslegacycookbooks.com), testing new recipes, and writing and publishing non-fiction books – half of which are cookbooks.

She finds great satisfaction and joy in sharing all she has learned with you, her readers, and hopes that you will benefit and develop a passion for cooking as great or greater than hers.

OTHER BOOKS BY THIS AUTHOR

Mama's Legacy Series

Seven Volumes Available

Dinner – 55 Easy Recipes (Volume I)

Breakfast and Brunch – 60 Delicious Recipes (Volume II)

Dessert – 50 Scrumptious Recipes (Volume III)

Chicken – 25 Classic Dinners (Volume IV)

Mexican Favorites – 21 Traditional Recipes (Volume V)

Side Dishes – 60 Great Recipes (Volume VI)

Sauce Recipes – 50 Tasty Choices (Volume VII)

Other Cookbooks

Candy Making Made Easy - Instructions and 17 Starter Recipes

Cake Making Made Easy - Instructions and 60 Cakes

Cook Ahead – Freezer to Table

Garden Fresh Soups and Stews

Juicing for Life – The Secret to Vibrant Health

SPECIAL DIETS Fresh and Easy Cookbook

Sweet Treats – Candy, Cookies, Cake, Ice Cream, Pudding, and Pie

Tweens and Teens – A Cookbook to Get You Started

COOKIES! The Best Collection of Cookie Recipes EVER! Just for YOU!

Health and Fitness/Gardening

DETOX – The Master Cleanse Diet

Growing Tomatoes – Everything You Need to Know, and More

Growing Roses – The Beginner's Handbook

Stop Eating Yourself into an Early Grave

WOW! You Look Fantastic!

Business

Attitude Adjustment

Starting an Online Business

Congratulations, You Are Self-Employed

Books Written under Pseudonyms

Power Up Your Brain – Five Simple Strategies (J. J. Jackson)

Clicker Training for Dogs (Amy Ellsworth)

Making Money with Storage Unit Auctions (Bryce Cranston)

www.ingramcontent.com/pod-product-compliance
Lightning Source LLC
Chambersburg PA
CBHW081543040426
42448CB00015B/3209